If I Could Leave One Book

Reflections Cultivating Peace of Mind

Jeff Tarumianz

To be identified with your mind is to be trapped in time: the compulsion to live almost exclusively through memory and anticipation. This creates an endless preoccupation with past and future and an unwillingness to honor and acknowledge the present moment and *allow it to be.* The compulsion arises because the past gives you an identity and the future holds the promise of salvation, of fulfillment in whatever form. Both are illusions.

Eckhart Tolle – *The Power of Now*

To the Reader:

This book originally was intended to pass as much wisdom to my children as possible, wisdom mostly learned through suffering and finding my way out. I then realized this book likely can benefit anyone interested in self-reflection and contemplation as an avenue to live a more serene and joyful life.

The key tools in my quest for emotional and spiritual health have been a consistent meditation practice, prayer, self-reflection and contemplation, the 12-steps, occasional stints of cognitive therapy, and much reading.

You will note the reflections are about me and my experiences. I don't like telling people what they should do, nor do I like when people tell me what to do; therefore, I keep the reflections about me.

I recommend pausing at the end of each reading and reflecting on what in your life might relate to the passage. Otherwise, the book might not be worth reading. The index should be helpful if you are looking for a particular topic. By the end, you will notice themes, but I think resemblance between some passages can only help if each is truly pondered in the context of one's own life.

Lastly, feel free to replace the words Higher Power/Creator/God/Universe with whatever identifier works for you. Generally speaking, I hope you will take what you like in the book and leave the rest.

Thank you to John Shukwit and Tait Arend for proofreading the manuscript. And to John Amen for providing thematic advice. Lastly, a special thank you to my wife, Liz, and children, Edwards and Ella, for being loving and real.

Jeff Tarumianz

Dear Edwards and Ella,

I have felt compelled for some time to write a book for you sharing what I have learned over the last 13 years from an emotional and spiritual standpoint. To put it bluntly, I did not have much health in these areas until I was 30 years old and started to seek it. I likely looked mostly fine to the outside world, but I needed and wanted more peace, serenity, and joy inside.

As your father, I will not be able to prevent painful experiences in your life, but I wanted to share many of the spiritual and emotional lessons I have learned so they may be of help when you navigate your own difficult experiences. Everyone faces challenges, and I hope this book might lessen the depth of anguish they can potentially cause. I love you so much.

Dad

Waiting for Happiness

"I'll be happy when…" likely is the biggest lie in the universe. It is an incredible source of pain. "I'll be happy when I have $X in the bank" or "when this loved one quits doing this" or "when I have a different boss," is a complete mirage. One can fill in the blank…this way of thinking is endless. Happiness comes from within, and thankfully, we have the tools to be happy regardless of our circumstances. It's not always easy, but it is possible.

Staying "Right-sized"

True humility, for me, is understanding that I am no
better or worse than any other human being and that
God (not me) is in charge. People have different
skills and weaknesses, but no one is "better" than
anyone else. Along these lines, I think our Creator
has the same love for everyone.

Fear Breeds Obsession

For a long time, many of my actions were driven, in a large part, by fear. I think the biggest problem with fear is that it can lead to an obsessive mind. If harnessed appropriately and dealt with calmly before it turns into obsession, fear actually can be a good tool/pointer where action needs to be taken.

Cleaning out my Closet

I believe if I can remove obstacles within myself that drag me down (i.e. self-defeating behaviors and coping mechanisms that no longer work) and be centered in my mind, body and spirit, then creativity can be unleashed, and the sky is the limit.

There are a lot of spiritual concepts out there that are great but don't really provide much healing unless I first have cut out my self-defeating behaviors. I had to find ways to get rid of defensiveness, judgment, resentment, people-pleasing, shame, invulnerability and fear for me to be clear of habitual ways of thinking that were dragging me down. I believe everyone has character traits that bring them down. Working to remove them is difficult but frees up the mind. Working the twelve steps with a sponsor has been the most effective tool for me.

Big Love

I believe our Creator loves us in ways words cannot express and wants us to love ourselves and others the same way. Only when I love and accept myself while maintaining humility can I truly love and accept others.

Following Passions and Talents

If I were to give my 17-year-old-self advice on vocation, it would be as follows: follow your passions and your dreams; use and develop your God given gifts and talents. We all inherit different gifts, talents, passions and purposes for a reason. If you don't cultivate yours, it will be hard to be fulfilled. If you can find your passion and purpose, and use it to serve God and others, you will live a big life.

The Root of Suffering

I suffer when I am attached to "my way" of how things "should be". There are countless attachments, but I think they all fall under the umbrella of how I want and expect the Universe to unfold.

Because I have a "my way", my mind tends to judge and label everything that happens as "good" or "bad". When something is "good", I cling to it and don't want it to change. When something is "bad", I resist it even though it is the way it is. I create suffering in both instances.

If I can release "my way", then I have fewer attachments and thereby judge, cling, and resist less, which increases my serenity.

Suffering and Attachment

The previous page is so critical to peace of mind, I have added this writing as another way of looking at the message. If I want to quit suffering, I must stop wanting things to be different than the way they are. There will be pain, and there will be options and choices in the face of pain. As long as I accept the reality of the situation and stop wishing it to be different, then I can move forward and through the pain without suffering.

I have a tendency to cling to what feels good and resist what feels bad. In this sense, I want things to stay the same when "good" and be different when "bad". Everything is always changing so I cannot keep something exactly the same nor can I force many things to be different than they are.

Awareness, Acceptance, Action

Acceptance does not mean letting other people treat me badly. There is no upside to knowingly accepting abusive situations. Acceptance might be better phrased as non-resistance. I cannot change something that has already happened, but I can keep my peace of mind by not resisting it and then taking the appropriate action. Sometimes the appropriate action will take courage and upset others, but that does not mean it is not the right action.

Conflict and Struggle

Conflict is a part of life. Fighting and struggling do not have to be. There are productive ways to handle conflict. To me, learning assertive communication is the best way to effectively handle conflict. Passive, aggressive, and passive-aggressive styles do not lead to progress. In my experience, only assertive and healthy communication does.

Forgiveness is for Me

Forgiveness is incredibly freeing. I had to learn that forgiveness does not mean accepting injurious behavior and walking right back into the same situation. I can forgive someone and not go back to the same dynamic. In this sense, forgiveness really is for myself and can set me free.

I had to learn true humility and compassion for the other person before I could learn to forgive. One of the most effective ways for me to build this compassion was to pray for the other person until the resentment against him/her had dissipated. There is a "resentment prayer" in 12-step circles where I pray for the one I resent to have health, happiness and anything he/she would want out of life, just like I would. I suspect many people holding onto resentments cannot bring themselves to do this.

As long as I cannot forgive the other person, I am chained to that person whether he/she is around me anymore or not. In this sense, "resentment is the poison I drink hoping the other person will die" is an incredibly meaningful quote for me.

Learning from Experts

If I want to grow and improve in certain areas of my life, I must seek out experts in the field in question. I try to seek out those who embody what I want. I wouldn't ask someone who has never been self-employed how to start a business; I wouldn't ask someone who has been married five times for marital advice. These are more obvious examples, but this simple concept can be overlooked. Thankfully, many experts are willing to share about their experience in their given field if I just ask.

Perception of God

I have heard the following put in different ways but strongly believe it - We will embody the traits we believe the God of our understanding has. If I believe in a distant, judgmental, shaming and punishing God, these characteristics will manifest in me. The effects of this and the corresponding ways I treat myself and others can be incredibly painful. It seems to make much more sense to get really close to a loving, caring and compassionate God.

Defining God

I don't think anyone really knows exactly who or what God is. If there are 7+ billion people on the earth, I am pretty sure there are 7+ billion perceptions of God. Too often we get hung up on wanting to define exactly who or what God is and then believe we are the only ones that know.

The important part for me is having faith in a power greater than myself and continuously strengthening my bond with this Higher Power. The characteristics of the Higher Power are also of critical importance, as described on the previous page. The more expansive my perception of God, the more expansive my life is. Keeping the faith in this loving God in the difficult times has been critical for me.

My Part

I try to hold myself responsible for being loving, kind, honest, humble, courageous, compassionate, empathic, and other life affirming qualities towards others. I am not responsible for, nor can I control, other people's thoughts, feelings and behaviors even if they want to make me responsible for them. Trying to manipulate or otherwise shape other's thoughts, feelings and actions is crazy making.

Value of Health

It has become very important for me to stay healthy in four key areas of my life that encompass my entire being: physical, mental, emotional and spiritual. If one of these areas is neglected, it is hard for me to be whole and in balance. When all four areas are strong, life tends to be fulfilling and a mostly exciting journey. This is when I can best rely on my intuition as well.

Happiness Building Blocks

If I were to propose a formula for happiness, it would be the following:

Humility + Gratitude + Compassion + Kindness to others = Happiness

If I had to choose one key to happiness, it would be gratitude.

Life can be Difficult

I don't think life is supposed to be easy nor is it about trying to arrange everything so that it is. I really thought it was for a long time. I learned the hard way that trying to avoid painful experiences at all costs is exhausting and leads to fear and mental anguish.

It also helps me to remember everyone goes through hard times, events, challenges, struggles etc. and what we make of them and how we respond ends up defining our life and our happiness to a large degree. Some have loved ones die too soon, some have debilitating accidents or diseases, some battle childhood traumas, some battle addiction, some go bankrupt...the list is endless. Realizing that life is not about avoiding all of this allows me to move through and process these trials and tribulations and grow stronger.

Upside to Pain

I believe even really painful events in life can have benefits. It's hard to see them when they are happening, but at some point, down the road, they will become clear. It may sound trite, but there really are lessons in everything. Remembering this when I am in the midst of a painful experience can help me keep hope and peace of mind.

Tool for Looking Inside

If someone does something that hooks my ego and I start getting all self-righteous, then the same thing likely is inside of me and I am resisting it. If I don't get all self-righteous, but the trait in the other person still bothers me, then there likely is something tangential to this trait in me that is unresolved.

For example, I really did not like when people would blame me for something I had no part in. I don't think this necessarily meant that I was a blamer, but I did find that I was overly responsible and took on the blame and felt the associated guilt even if I did nothing wrong.

Keeping it Real

It's helpful for me to understand and remember that no matter what I am going through, someone always has it worse. This is not an excuse to accept harmful or degrading situations, a reason for inaction, or to say I should not feel pain, but it can help keep things in perspective. It helps me to take note when someone else is going through something unfortunate because I can be compassionate and empathetic towards them and realize my struggles aren't as bad as I think they are.

Why me?

Asking "why me?" does not serve any purpose from
what I can tell. Nor does believing and proclaiming
something is "not fair." Things will happen to
everyone that they never imagined would. As soon as
I can move away from a victim mentality to
acceptance of what happened and do what I can
about it, the better off I am.

Connection to God

The more in touch I am with God, the better my life seems to be. Days where I think about God go much better, compared to days when I don't. Days where I try to connect with God throughout the day go much better than the ones where I just think of God once in the morning.

Desire to Control

Things don't seem to go well when I try to make the world be what I want it to be. Usually, I will try to force things with my self-will and forget the world is bigger than I am. As alluded to earlier in the book, if there is a "my way", there will be suffering.

Choosing a Response

When I can deliberately respond to situations rather than reacting, things go much smoother. When I start feeling pressure building inside my body and start thinking that I may combust if I don't act immediately, I need to bite my tongue and let the pressure subside. When I succumb to the temptation to act immediately/react, the result is rarely, if ever, productive.

Crappy Behavior

People behaving badly towards others probably are not feeling good about themselves. This may be easier to live with in the adult world compared to the bullying of children, but I think it can be helpful to understand this regardless of age. "Hurt people hurt people" has been a helpful adage for me to remember.

This does not mean we should accept unacceptable behavior, but it helps to realize the other person likely is in some pain and acting out from it. He/she likely is not feeling much love, nor does he/she know how to ask for it in healthy ways. It helps me to remember this so I can choose to love them instead of getting defensive or put off by their behavior.

Evaluating Criticism

Criticism is hard, but if I can learn to make use of it, I will be better served. People's criticisms don't always have merit. Other times they do. If, in these cases, I do not judge myself and understand I am not less of a person, I can apply the criticism to make myself a better and happier person. If more than one person has the same criticism of me, it probably makes that much more sense to look at it. Of course, a consensus does not always mean something is "right".

Choosing Friends

I like the quotes I hear telling me to surround myself with people I want to be like. This message often is framed as if I want insight into myself, I should look at the 5 people I spend the most time with. It also helps me to remember these 5 people might be different depending on which facet of my life is in question.

Defining Love

I think "Love" is too nebulous of a term for
something so integral to a joyful life. It helps me to
think of the components of love being acceptance,
affection, attention and appreciation. These are
tangible actions I can practice making love grow in
my life. And who wouldn't want to be the recipient of
these? I first heard these components of love from
Deepak Chopra.

Taking a Stand

Standing up to wrongs/injustices is a good thing and seems to have lost some of its value at some point. A key to this is knowing what truly is an injustice. My ego or conditioned mind can color an event or situation as "wrong" based on my past experiences and biases. Often, these may not be "wrongs". There are other times when injustices are obvious and undeniable. Great people in history often are great because they stood up to true injustices.

Mind-Body Connection

Exercise seems to greatly benefit my mental well-being in addition to the more obvious physical benefits. I think the mental aspect is often overlooked. This further convinces me that the body, mind and soul are incredibly interconnected. If one is suffering, the others will also.

Difficult People

It helps me to remember that people are not their behaviors and that everyone is doing the best they can. I try to love people and address behaviors. Sometimes it calls for boundaries and potentially distance, but if I can always practice compassion, then I can be happy with my own behavior.

Value of Stillness

There are numerous benefits of being able to sit quietly with myself for an extended period of time. They include, but are not limited to, more peace of mind, serenity, and seeing the truth.

It seems modern life is not very conducive to stillness. I try to beware of society's pressures to be a "human doing" rather than a human being. A lot of people seem to be just going and going and going and spreading themselves too thin. I believe rest and recovery are incredibly important to living a fulfilling life, and spending some time in stillness is critical.

Thinking vs. Action

The lessons in this book are not worth a whole lot unless they are put into action. Otherwise it is just information. For years, I fell into the trap of trying to think my way out of difficult situations. I likely unconsciously believed that if I could figure out why something was the way it was, it would change the situation at hand. Action must occur in addition to contemplation for anything to really change or get better.

I also need to remember that sometimes I cannot change things. I like the Buddhist maxim saying "I can not understand, and things will be as they are. I can understand, and things will be as they are."

Focusing on Others

I find that when I am obsessing about something, it is rarely about me or something I can control. It is almost always about someone else and what they are doing, how they are behaving, and/or something I am fearing. Many of the tools in this book can get me out of obsessing if I choose to use them (e.g. go exercise, journal, meditate, pray, talk to a trusted advisor, work a 12-step program, etc.).

Wanting

I am beginning to believe that I have exactly what I need at all times. It just depends if I choose to quit wanting more or for things to be different.

Was it Really all Me?

I believe everything I have accomplished and been blessed with has been through God. When I remember this, life flows with a lot less angst and struggle. My ego might like to say how great and smart I am, but any success that comes to me has been first enabled by God/Higher Power.

Cueing into Control

If I find myself telling others "you should or shouldn't do this or that" or "you need to do this or that" because I don't approve of their current actions, there is a good chance I have a control issue/problem.

Another warning is when I find myself saying the same thing over and over to someone or trying to change the message slightly, so it will finally sink in. If this is the case, then I am trying to control something I have no control over.

Relieving Suffering

I am convinced an absolute miracle for anyone suffering mental, emotional or spiritual anguish is a 12-step program. There is a lot of anguish in this world that has been alleviated where science has no answer. A 12-step program seems like a good option for anyone who wants to take their spirituality and mental and emotional well-being to a whole new level. It's easy for people to say they don't qualify, but everyone who has a relative or friend that is an alcoholic qualifies for Al Anon. Seems like a wide net.

Processing Feelings

I have learned the importance of accurately identifying my feelings and feeling them. Emotional issues will creep up when I don't let myself feel feelings.

Thoughts give rise to feelings which give rise to behaviors. I don't think we can control the thoughts that pop into our heads...the randomness of thoughts confirms this for me. Furthermore, I cannot control the feelings that arise from thoughts, so I try to consciously watch my thoughts and feel my feelings without judging myself.

Processing thoughts and feelings and then consciously choosing an action is paramount for me living an emotionally healthy life. A consistent meditation practice has been the best way for me to develop these skills.

Playing Small and Safe

It's hard to learn anything new if I am not willing to step out of my comfort zone.

Soul Killers

I think shame likely is the top soul killer, followed by
guilt, resentment, victimization and blame.

Traits of Gratitude

Gratitude does not include turning a blind eye to bad things that may happen. It does include remembering what I am grateful for in both good times and bad.

Community

It has become important for me to surround myself
with people who love me. I also believe it's wise to
look out for people who say they love you but in
reality, don't treat you lovingly...actions very much
speak louder than words when it comes to love. It's
important for me to find and surround myself with
those who treat me lovingly, truly want the best for
me and want to see me flourish.

Acceptance and Courage

Acceptance is essentially non-resistance...not resisting what is and acting when needed is a path to serenity and peace of mind. I think it's important to take a stand when something is not acceptable. I try not to resist it, because it has happened, but I need to summon the courage to stand up when it is not acceptable.

Learning Vulnerability

I have learned to be vulnerable with people I can be vulnerable with and not be vulnerable with those I cannot be. I am not vulnerable with people who have proven they will judge me or use the thoughts and feelings I share with them against me.

What I Can Control

When I understand what I can and cannot control and when I align my energies accordingly, life flows. I believe I can control my actions and not much else. I cannot control my thoughts and the feelings that arise, but I can control my actions and behaviors that result from them if I am conscious of what the thoughts and feelings are. I cannot control other people, places and things, but I can control my response to them.

Compassion

I believe all humans have character shortcomings or
self-defeating behaviors. I have tried to identify mine,
pray for relief from them and practice their opposites.
It helps me be compassionate towards others when I
remember we all have shortcomings that have
developed since birth, simply by being human.
Those who become truly aware and awake to theirs
are the lucky ones in my opinion.

Intuition vs. Instincts

If I am clear of self-defeating behaviors, I feel like my intuition is God speaking to me. Not my instincts but rather my intuition. My intuition comes from the gut rather than the head. It seems to arise from a creative place or space. This is why it is important to be still and quiet and listen to my intuition...this is different than quickly following my instincts, which are more likely to be knee-jerk responses based on past conditioning.

Calming the Mind

My mind races a lot less and my sleep has improved since beginning a dedicated meditation practice. I suspect the more the mind has been running life, the longer it takes meditation to reverse the effects. But, peace comes incrementally, over time, and is more than well worth the effort.

Stress

Stressors in life will happen, but I think we can go through life without stress/distress. Eustress helps us grow, but we can do this without the anxious, frenetic feeling that distress brings. This book, in a large part, is about minimizing distress.

Needing Help

I believe everyone is struggling with something most of the time. Unfortunately, there seems to be societal pressure convincing us not to talk about it.

For a long time, I thought I was supposed to be entirely self-sufficient, grin and bear everything, pull myself up by my bootstraps, and never be "needy". Resilience is hugely important, but I cannot overcome some things without sharing my experience and asking for help. Something tells me the Universe will continue to present me with challenges until I admit I cannot do it all on my own. Giving myself permission to need help at times has been a substantive part of my growth.

The Ultimate Motivator

I don't think there is any motivator quite like pain and suffering. Every time I have had profound advances in my spiritual and emotional health, they have been preceded by relatively intense pain and suffering. Only when I surrendered, did a shift occur. I had to accept the fact that my perceived solutions did not work, and it was futile to keep trying. In this sense, I always relate to the saying "surrender to win". I now try to practice surrender before the suffering comes.

Parenting

It might be too early to know what stereotypes my children's generation will be painted with, but the preceding one (Millennials) has been said to have been too coddled. My hope is that I have been balanced in showing my children both love and discipline. Love undoubtedly is the most powerful action in the universe. Entitlement, on the other hand, keeps us stuck. I hope I have taught them that things are not going to be handed to them. I also hope that I have taught them that unchecked self-will and determination can cause pain too.

Technology

All of this being "wired" in the information age can be dangerous. Humans are meant to live in the moment and live balanced lives. Multi-tasking and being glued to electronics leave no room for being present, much less available to God. It is easy to see that for some people it has become another way to avoid sitting with their feelings.

Dissecting Anger

Anger arises when an expectation is not met. I think
it is important to check the expectation to see if it is
reasonable or not...many times it is not. There often
is something underlying anger, whether it's fear or
sadness or another feeling...not always, but often.
The anger that is not a result of an underlying
emotion often can be used as a sign pointing to action
that needs to be taken.

It also has been helpful for me to realize that
oftentimes when I am angry about something, I
actually am angry at myself for not taking a certain
action that likely would have prevented the situation
at hand from happening. I try to be forgiving of
myself, learn from the situation and not take the anger
out on others.

Self-Care

I try to give from overflow. After years of horrible self-care, I realized I must take care of myself and fill myself up, so I can give from overflow. Ironically, I tended to be more self-centered in my thoughts but not actions when I was taking poor care of myself. I have nothing to give or offer to others if I am depleted. Putting the oxygen mask on one's self in a plane before helping the child, is a great metaphor for this.

Nutrition

I think it is unfortunate what we have done to our food supply. I wish processed foods, preservatives, and refined sugars were not so prevalent. I recently came across the book *The 150 Healthiest Foods on Earth* by Jonny Bowden. It seems like a diet of these foods would be a smart way to eat and give the body a good chance of feeling good.

Finding a Partner

I think it's important to choose a significant other that loves you how you want to be loved instead of choosing someone based on what you know or what has been modeled for you.

My hope for my children is that they find a significant other who speaks kindly to them, wants what is best for them, encourages them to be vulnerable with him/her, is compassionate towards them, does not judge them, supports them following their dreams and wants to grow as a person each day. I also hope he/she can help them see self-defeating behaviors in a loving way to help them become a better person. Lastly, I love the advice of listing out the qualities we want in a partner and then embodying them ourselves. We attract what we are, so the best way to attract a loving significant other is to be loving.

Love and Acceptance

It's hard to be loving and accepting towards others if we are not loving and accepting towards ourselves first.

Finding Happiness

I am convinced we don't need material possessions to live a happy life. In fact, when I make a list of what truly makes me happy, everything I value actually costs nothing. I find it comforting that happiness does not come through attaining wealth, possessions, status or superiority/control.

Abundance

I believe God gives me everything I truly need and
will continue to do so; therefore, I might as well get
out of fear of not having enough, find my passion and
not compromise. This might be the best way to find
abundance.

Helping Others

It is important to me to share my resources when I have more than enough. I also believe what seems to have been proven scientifically in that serving others leads to happiness.

Goodwill towards Others

When I can genuinely be happy for the good fortune
of others, my own life tends to unfold more smoothly
with less tension. Thinking about how others don't
"deserve" something good that happened to them
only weighs me down.

Seeds of Joy

If there is a magic bullet for happiness it probably is gratitude. I think service to others likely is next. If I can be grateful for all of God's gifts, help others, and remain humble, life is rich. By humble, I mean remembering that I am no better or worse than anyone else and that God is in charge. I believe God is in me and everyone else just the same, and we are all wonderful yet small compared to God. And by helping others, I mean acts of kindness in large quantities. It doesn't have to be something ground-breaking; it can be opening the door for someone, smiling at someone, giving a word of encouragement, etc.

A Universe that Humbles

It seems that every time I start to think I know how to do things better than someone else or I have it all figured out, some pain comes my way to humble me and show me I don't know, nor will I never know, it all. This phenomenon is uncanny.

Living Life

I love the following quote from the movie Shawshank Redemption…. "Either get busy living or get busy dying". It seems we all are doing one of the two. I benefit from occasionally checking in with this quote in relation to the life I am living to make sure I am living in a way I want.

The "My Way" Continuum

Resentment is about not getting what I wanted in the past. Anger is about not getting what I want in the present. Fear is the thought of not getting what I want in the future.

The tighter I clasp to "my way", the more I will swim in toxic emotions, hence the more suffering I will find.

Expectations

It has been critical for me to learn realistic and fair expectations. I think it is OK to have some expectations, but they can be a slippery slope. For me it really comes down to expecting people to not physically, mentally or emotionally abuse me or others. I think if I did not have these expectations, then I would not stand up to anything. Any expectations beyond this typically cause me agony and may as well be premeditated resentments.

Importance of Grieving

I have found there are times in life when I need to grieve. Bottling it up and putting it on a shelf caused serious pain before I learned this. Sometimes the grief is so intense, allowing myself to feel the pain and cry for as long as my body needs is the most cathartic action I can take.

To Thine Own Self Be True

I think it's important to not let other people tell me
who I am and what I am not. No one knows me better
than I do. I have learned to trust my gut, especially
when I am free of the effects of any self-defeating
behaviors and can tune into my intuition. I have had
enough examples where I went against my gut and
something did not work out to know I need to take
the time to listen to it and honor it.

Giving Away My Power

I try not to attach my peace of mind to other people's choices, feelings, behaviors or words.

Accurate Language

I have tried to become more conscious when describing feelings and beliefs. For example, "I feel like you don't care about me" is a belief, not a feeling. "I feel sad because I think you don't care about me" is a way to express a feeling and a belief. Confusing feelings and beliefs in a relationship, along with the language that goes with it, often will lead to unproductive communication.

More Language to Notice

I have found it helps to pay attention to language to check in with how I or another person is truly feeling.

"You hurt my feelings" likely is another way of saying "I got sad when you treated me that way, and it makes me feel too vulnerable to tell you I am sad." The second way is not blaming or victim inducing and more productive in relationship.

Another example of saying something while meaning something else is "I'll let you do that" instead of saying "I am overwhelmed and need help, but I am not comfortable being vulnerable and admitting I need help."

In these respects, I think it is important for me to say what I mean, mean what I say, and not say it mean.

Giving to Give

I have found it is important for me to be kind and giving with absolutely no strings attached. Even spiritual reasoning of "more will come back to me" is a string attached. Sometimes the strings attached are quite subtle, but I think happiness is increased only if the act is truly selfless.

Labeling and Judging

For whatever reason, we humans feel the need to put a label on just about everything. "That person is mean and crazy...That person is nice but not very smart." I think it can be helpful to recognize unskilled behavior in others, but as soon as any judgment is added (often coming with a hint of self-righteousness and lack of humility) then I am damaging my own happiness. I think people often don't make the connection because it can give one a little hit of feeling good before the negative effects take hold.

Accepting Others

Constant focus on others' behavior leads to a lot of pain. I must let others be who they are if I want any chance at happiness. I try to make it a point to not let others mistreat me or others, but otherwise, I try to let them be who they are. A lot of angst can be eliminated by doing so. And, I am not sure there is a greater gift to give someone.

Victimization

I don't think anything keeps people stuck more than settling into a victim role and blaming others. When someone takes an action that I don't like, it might make me feel a certain way, but it is important for me to remember that I am responsible for my feelings, processing them and then behaving in a certain way. When I blame someone else for my feelings, I have given my personal power and freedom of choice away. This victim mentality is a guaranteed way to stay stuck and unhappy.

"Negative" Emotions

I am not sure there is anything wrong with anger or other so-called negative emotions like guilt and fear if noticed quickly. Problems arise when we do not keep these emotions in check by way of processing them and moving on. Anger can be a signal that I need to take an action or make a stand against something. Guilt is useful because it is a signal that I might need to apologize to someone for behaving in a way that is not acceptable. Fear can alert me to stay away from a situation that is truly dangerous. I believe these feelings or emotions were given by our Creator. Learning how to work with them is what is important because difficulties will no doubt arise when these emotions are not managed well.

Another Stab at Acceptance

I try to practice non-resistance, non-attachment and non-judgement. I think this practice is the true ticket to peace and serenity. It is and will forever be a continuous practice for me, and the human condition provides ample opportunities to practice.

Non-resistance does not mean inaction but rather not fighting or struggling against something that has happened and is now in the unchangeable past.

Non-attachment does not mean a cold, detached posture in relationships but rather not having to have things be a certain way for me to be at peace. I would argue a true and pure love can only occur from a place of non-attachment. We tend to attach not just to people but also places, things and ideas. At the end of the day, all attachments probably could be classified in terms of our ideas of how we want things to be.

Non-judgement is about observing our outer and inner worlds without having to label everything as "good" or "bad".

Processing Anger

Healthy anger management is not easy but crucial for our health and our relationships. Sometimes people offload their anger, which can bring psychological damage to the targets. Others may stuff the anger, which leads to corrosive resentment that can come out sideways in unproductive ways. I tended to stuff anger and other feelings for a long time. It has been important for me to learn to feel anger, process it, be conscious of it dissipating, let it go and then act if necessary.

Working Hard

I am not sure there is any way around hard work if
there is a goal I want to meet. Vision and intention
are necessary, but I don't think they alone can achieve
desired outcomes. My tendency has been to look for
the short cut, but at the end of the day, successes I
have enjoyed required hard work.

As Sick as Our Secrets

If I am disturbed and my head is spinning about
something, I need to share this with someone. It also
can help to journal about what I am going through
before I share it with someone else. The disturbance
and related events will lose their power if I go through
this process. This might be another way of saying we
are only as sick as our secrets.

Negative Payoffs

Fear gets me going in the head.
Resentment keeps me up at night.
Arrogance prevents me from having real relationships.
Shame keeps me from acknowledging the truth.

Trust and Faith

I try to remind myself that my Higher Power always takes care of me when I allow this to be the case. All I must do is trust my Higher Power <u>now</u> and have faith that my Higher Power will care for me in the <u>future</u>.

Irritation as a Guide

When I am bothered, my character shortcomings/self-defeating behaviors likely are flaring up (e.g. judgment, resentment, shame, fear, etc.). If this is not the case, then it is almost guaranteed I am wanting someone else to be or act differently, and a desire to control the other person has arisen. Most often, when I am struggling, both dynamics are present.

God in Everyone

When I can remember that God is in me and in everyone else, anxiety, friction with others, and general struggle decrease dramatically.

Thoughts on Money

The best money strategy for me has been to spend
some, save some for retirement and give some away.
The more I get, the more I can give away which is
important for me. It probably goes without saying
that money can be incredibly dangerous without
balance. If I become a miser and store it all up, then I
will be miserable. If I spend it all in profligate ways,
then I will be miserable.

Another helpful viewpoint for me was hearing money
described as energy (Mastin Kipp). For me it
validates why I should use some, save some for a later
date and give some to others that don't have even the
least bit of it/energy.

More on Grieving

Learning to grieve has been an important part of my emotional growth. If I don't grieve heartbreaking events, I will continue to find distractions to divert my attention from my sadness and pain. I have seen it in others as well and have come to believe not grieving when it is needed leads to being addicted to something: alcohol, gambling, shopping, sugar, drama...anything to preoccupy the mind as opposed to facing and fully feeling the heartbreak.

God's Will

I tend to want solutions to problems immediately.
Solutions seem to come more on God's time.
However, I have learned that if I am patient and listen
for God's will, then I will be given guidance on the
next right course of action. For this to work, I need to
ask God for His will via prayer and listen for the
answer via stillness and meditation. Unfortunately, if
I am carrying around a bunch of emotional baggage,
then I will hear my will and mistake it for God's.

Guilt in Relationships

I found that at times avoiding guilt kept me locked into unhealthy relationships. I delayed changing my part in these relationships for fear of the guilt I might have to face if my changes made the other person unhappy. Until I face and resolve these feelings inside me and act authentically, I cannot have a relationship that embodies a healthy non-attachment and true love.

Fear vs. Gratitude

For some reason, it is hard for me to remember, but the best way for me to combat unhealthy fear is through gratitude and appreciation. Fear subsides when I consciously ponder what I have to be grateful for.

I recently came across the following advice from Tony Robbins, which I totally buy: "When you trade expectation for appreciation, your whole world changes in an instant." A similar quote I have heard is "The struggle ends when gratitude begins." (Neale Donald Walsch).

Trust and Action

I recently heard and liked the maxim of "Trust God, but tie up your camel". Sometimes I want to sit back, take no action and let the world be, but for life to flow, I still must take appropriate action when needed. Like the serenity prayer, I must trust God with things out of my control and take necessary action when needed along the lines of God's will and leave the outcome up to God.

Serenity Prayer: "God, grant me the serenity to accept the things I cannot change, the courage to change the things I can, and the wisdom to know the difference."

What is Not God's Will

If I think I am doing God's will but I am judging someone, trying to control them or otherwise fight with them, then I need to question my perception of the God I am worshipping.

People-Pleasing

As someone who has battled people-pleasing, it is important for me to check in with whose approval I am seeking. While it can seem selfless and noble on the surface, if I am acting just to please someone, then it is not a loving act. There is a string attached that is self-centered because I am thinking about the way the act will make me feel. True love and acts of kindness have no strings attached.

Buying into Stories

When I find myself using the words "always" or "never" (especially in an argument), I am in a story I have manufactured and really want to believe.

Perfectionism

I have heard perfectionism is the highest form of self-abuse, and I believe it. I think often it is developed in an effort to avoid feeling bad about oneself.

Conflict Management

I have found no better guide to conflict management and resolution than Pages 199-201 of <u>The Dance with Anger</u>. It is best read from Harriett Lerner's book for additional context, but the core steps are below...

1. Do speak up when an issue is important to you.
2. Don't strike while the iron is hot.
3. Do take time to think about the problem and to clarify your position.
4. Don't use "below-the-belt" tactics.
5. Do speak in "I" language.
6. Don't make vague requests.
7. Do try to appreciate people are different.
8. Don't participate in intellectual arguments that go nowhere.
9. Do recognize that each person is responsible for his or her own behavior.
10. Don't tell another person what she or he thinks or "should" think or feel.
11. Do try to avoid speaking through a third-party.
12. Don't expect change to come about from hit-and-run confrontations.

Growth

It seems to me that a constant pursuit of learning tends to bode well for people.

Judging Others

I did not realize it for a long time but judging
someone else only hurts me. When I pay attention to
the way I feel inside when judging someone else, it is
not a pleasant feeling.

It is helpful for me to recognize, observe and discern
unskilled behavior in others, but the moment I start to
judge others and think I am somehow better or
smarter, then my humility has gone out the door.
Everyone is doing the best they can, and no one is
perfect.

Letting Others Feel

It's hard to connect with someone if I am telling them they should not feel one way or another. A good example is if someone says they are fearful about something and I say that is silly. While it may not seem like a legitimate worry, it is what the other person is feeling so to them there is realness to it. This is where it helps for me to listen nonjudgmentally and not take things personally if I really want to connect and have a healthy and loving exchange.

Another Person's Anger

For a long time, I would have rather been hit by a
baseball bat in the stomach than have someone close
to me angry with me. I had to learn to let people have
their feelings no matter what they are. If I do
something wrong, I can apologize, know that I am
human, and try to correct it going forward. Beating
myself up does no good. There also are times when
people are mad and I don't owe amends for anything.
I just need to let them have their feelings and know
that there is a lot going on inside of them that has
nothing to do with me.

Foundation for Empathy

If I think I know the best way to do everything, then empathy is impossible. I first must have humility before I can build compassion for others, which then allows for empathy.

The Ego and Communication

I cannot have sincere communication with someone if my ego is involved. Whenever my ego is involved, I will take a stance that protects and attempts to strengthen my ego as opposed to listening to the other.

Feeling Discomfort

My mind will do a lot to avoid discomfort or feeling pain. It will focus on work, sing a song, look for a substance to change its course, or any other attempt at diversion. Feeling discomfort is part of life just like feeling happiness or anything else. Learning to sit with discomfort without reaching for something to take it away and until it passes has served me well.

Triggers

It has helped me to identify scenarios that trigger me due to past conditioning. This way I can notice them when they arise and know that there is more than just the present moment affecting the way I want to respond to something. As a result, I know that my instinctual response might not be warranted because I am seeing something with added baggage from the past. Some situations that trigger me and start to get me worked up are:

- Someone telling me what to do.
- Another person's anger.
- Hypocrisy.
- People setting their own rules/laws.
- People who think they are the center of the universe.
- Any type of shaming language.
- Blaming me for something I have nothing to do with.
- Someone not giving my feelings a second thought and turning everything around to them.
- Belittling something that I love and have worked hard at.
- Someone else making decisions for me.

Guaranteed Unhappiness

Waiting for someone to change so I can be happy is a one-way ticket to misery.

Whose Approval Do I Need?

Seeking the approval of others created a lot of pain in my life for a lengthy period of time. I finally realized God's approval and my own were far more important.

Letting Go of Resentment

I have found the best way for me to stop resenting someone is to pray for the other person for a few weeks until I feel compassion for him/her (common in 12-step circles). I pray that he/she would have everything I would want in life...peace, serenity and joy and that they have everything they might want in life. This is not easy in the beginning, but the relief gained over time is miraculous.

Anger and Expectations

Anger happens when things don't go according to my expectations. In this sense, it seems like a pretty self-centered emotion in most circumstances. There are cases where anger is justified, like standing up to abuse or bigotry for example. I think people classify too much as "justified" though.

Anger can be useful but is also dangerous. If I want to get angry at spilled milk, I can set my expectations that milk should not be spilled. If I don't want to be verbally abused, I can set my expectations that I will not be verbally abused, and I will get angry and stand up for myself if it happens. One example seems healthy to me and the other does not.

Banging My Head against the Wall

If I continually struggle with another person's actions/behaviors, then I likely have not surrendered to the fact that I cannot control the other person.

Possessions

I heard a friend of mine once mention "he who have cow, have care of cow". This has been an amazing tool for me to ask myself if I really want to acquire something in a world awash in consumerism. I have found I actually want very few "cows" due to the upkeep.

Dropping Judgment

Sometimes I wonder if I judge others to avoid some self-judgment that I know is around the corner. In this respect, I suspect if I no longer judge myself, then I will no longer judge others.

Focusing in the Right Place

I think the best thing I can do if I see something in someone that I don't like is to be compassionate towards the other and practice the opposite.

Roots of Anxiety

I find that anxiety arises from a need to control
things. If I give up the need for control, then I won't
have anxiety. Some people try to prevent anxiety by
making sure they can control everything around
them. This is a recipe for disaster and misery because
at some point something or someone comes along
that cannot be controlled.

Watching the Mind

I can't think of a more valuable skill I have learned
than watching my mind without identifying with it or
reacting to it. It's interesting in mediation to see my
mind's patterns when it reaches into the past or
future.

Learning to watch my mind allows me to not attach to
or identify with my thoughts. This way I can see
what is real and when I actually need to act on a
thought. Just because a thought pops into my head
doesn't mean it's true or that I must act on it.

What I can Control

I have learned I don't have control over what thoughts and feelings appear in my mind and body, but I do have control over how I respond/act/behave when they arise. At the same time, I must own my thoughts and feelings and not blame others for "making me feel" a certain way. They don't have control over the thoughts and feelings that arise in me and playing the victim role gives them power over how I feel.

The way I respond to something is the only thing I have control over. Perhaps I have some control over my attitude and beliefs, but one could say these are just thoughts we choose to hold dear. Nonetheless, some beliefs serve me far better than others.

Being an Example

I have learned through pain that I cannot change people. All I can do is be an example.

"Live and Let Live"

Other people have a right to their own journey, just like I do. I am not living my life when I am busy trying to live others' lives for them.

When to Give Up

I am not sure "never give up" is always the best advice. I do think giving up might be an art form and becoming savvy at it can lead to more fulfillment and less struggle. Lately I have been thinking the secret to giving up is to never give up trying to change things I can change for the better...whether it is my craft, my character, my hobby, etc. On the flipside, I need to always give up trying to change things I don't have control over...a customer's response, another person's behavior, etc. It's not always easy to see what I can change and have control over, so it is important for me to stop and think about it and then put my best foot forward. I also think it is important to know that all endeavors will experience setbacks, and it is critical for me to not give up at these junctures if it is something I am passionate about and improving upon.

Present Moment Awareness

The best way for me to be grounded in the present moment is to be actively looking for things to be grateful for in the present moment.

Present, Past and Future

I am not sure if it is possible to have peace, contentment and joy if I am not dwelling in the present. If I am in the past, I likely will have some form of guilt, remorse or resentment present, even if it is very subtle. If I am in the future, I likely will have some sort of anxiety or fear. In this sense, leaving the present moment and getting wrapped up in time is what creates suffering.

Addiction

There seems to be an immense amount of emotional dysfunction that comes along with addiction and environments that are breeding grounds for addiction. The denial associated with them sometimes makes this difficult to see.

Shaming Others

It has become clear to me that some people use shame to try to change another person's behavior. Usually, this is a last resort, but if proven effective, it can become a go-to for someone who wants to shape another person's behavior.

When someone says something shaming to me, it is important for me to understand that the other person is trying to change my behavior or otherwise control me. Most importantly, I must not take on the shame and tell myself I am a bad person. Many times, I find that I don't regret the way I have been behaving. If I do, then I can apologize and know that I still am not a bad person.

Shaming language can be overt or subtle. "Shame on you", "You know better than that", "You are ruining our family", "How could you do that?", "I knew I should not have trusted you", "What is wrong with you?", etc. are all examples of trying to get another to change by using shame. There really is no place for the recipient to go, if not equipped to navigate this, other than thinking he/she is not allowed to make mistakes and is less of a person/not worthy. I am not sure there is anything more cruel than shaming another human being.

Accepting Others

I think the most efficient and effective path to serenity might be accepting others for who they are.

This also seems like the most loving thing we can possibly do.

Taking Advice

I like the saying "don't draw me a map if you have never been there". I try to take someone's experience and motives into account when they are offering unsolicited advice.

Clear and Calm Thinking

Nothing allows me to think clearly and calmly more than a meditation practice.

Loving Others How They Want to be Loved

The best tool I have learned for strengthening a bond with a significant other is to ask her/him to fill in the blank to the following statement: "I feel the most loved when you......", and then act on it.

The answers might be a surprise, and it is the best way to know how to love the other in ways he/she truly feels loved.

HALT

I think the acronym HALT is great advice. I know when I am hungry, angry, lonely or tired, I am more likely to find myself in some sort of conflict that could have been prevented if I had just halted.

Checking My Motives

I have found it helps me to check my motives when I am contemplating taking an action. If my motives are even remotely selfish, something inevitably goes wrong or comes back to bite me if I do in fact act on the self-centered motive.

Conditional vs. Unconditional Love

While difficult to admit, I unfortunately loved others
conditionally for a long time. As long as they were
doing what I wanted them to do, then I could be
loving. The degree to which I loved was based on the
degree to which I approved of their actions. Once I
found some true humility, compassion, empathy, and
forgiveness, then I could let people be who they are
while loving them in a truer and consistent way.

Living in the Future

While I try to live in the present moment, I find my mind often going into the future. For some reason my mind doesn't trust that I will be "ok" in the future; therefore, I better strategize now on how I can line things up to meet my desires and thus be "ok". Maybe humans are hardwired to focus on survival, but I suspect this also is one of the ego's favorite self-preservation techniques. Coming back to the present moment and trusting that my Higher Power will give me what I need seems to be the best way to get out of it. Watching my mind with some curiosity and without judgment also helps because I can notice the noise for what it is.

The Ego

My ego is that which worries what others think of me.
My ego is that which needs to be right.
My ego is that which longs to be understood.
My ego is that which compares me to others.
My ego is that which judges and labels others.
My ego is that which thinks I do not have enough.
My ego is that which needs other people to be a
certain way.

I am not my ego.

Favorite Books

The books that have had the most impact on my quest for spiritual and emotional health are below. For anyone waking up in the morning thinking "wow, I am not living the life I wanted to live", I highly suggest reading these books in the order below.

What Happy People Know – Dan Baker
The Ultimate Happiness Prescription – Deepak Chopra
The Power of Now – Eckhart Tolle

A Way to Be

Whether or not one is a Christian, I think the New Testament is a great place to look for guidance on living a spiritual and fulfilling life. For example, when I read the Book of Matthew, some of the direction that comes to me is as follows:

- Stay humble.
- Be merciful.
- Hunger for justice.
- Do not pick fights.
- Love everyone.
- Give anonymously.
- Help others.
- Forgive.
- Do not hoard money and possessions.
- Trust that God will always provide.
- Do not worry.
- Do not judge others.
- Seek and love God.
- Be what you want others to be.
- Follow the lead of those doing good works.
- Seek and try to do God's will.
- Help the downtrodden.
- When you find heaven, you put all else down.
- Drop your ego.
- Love your neighbor as yourself.

My hopes for you, my children (Edwards and Ella):

My main hope is that you will live a mostly peaceful and joyous life. I don't think it is possible to always be happy, nor is it what we are intended to be. I think being human entails experiencing a range of emotions. But, I do think there is an ever-present joy and peace that can be lived no matter what feelings we are having or experiences or hardships we are moving through. My deepest wish for you is that you have this joy and peace that is always with you.

I hope that you live a healthy life from an emotional, spiritual, physical and mental level. This is not always easy and has taken dedication for me. There will be painful experiences in life, but I do believe much of suffering is optional. The healthier I am in these four areas, the better I can navigate life's trials and tribulations and also be appreciative of and have a deep gratitude for life.

I hope you will be kind and loving to yourself. No one is perfect and being unloving to yourself or shaming towards yourself is a one-way ticket to unhappiness. It was for me. It is hard to give and receive love if we can't do it to ourselves.

I hope you don't let other people tell you who you are or who you should be. I hope you have people in your life who can be honest and loving towards you at the same time…who can help you see any self-inflicted roadblocks and also be gentle with you. I hope you find people who support you and truly want what's best for you and take joy in seeing you thrive. Sometimes people don't want you to grow because they are afraid they will be left behind. Notice this and spread your wings, be true to yourself, and follow your dreams.

I hope you know how much I love you and how beautiful you are inside and out. I tell you so often how much I love you, how proud I am of you, and how God's love is so big for you that it is incomprehensible. You guys may get tired of hearing this, but these are the truest things I know.

I hope you will find an incredibly strong relationship with a Higher Power/God of your understanding. There is no doubt in my mind that the more expansive, loving and kind your Higher Power is, the more joyous and peaceful you will be. Again, I learned this the hard way, as you can see in the preceding pages.

I hope that if you choose to get married, you will find a spouse who is kind to you, loving towards you, patient with you, honest with you about everything, and supports you. I also think it is true that the more we can become the things we are looking for in a partner/spouse, the more likely we are to attract that type of person.

I hope that you find a vocation that you love and are passionate about. The difference between dreading going to work versus doing something you love is huge. I have experienced both, and it sure is nice to not have to prefer one day in the week more than another just by virtue of where it falls in the week's order.

Lastly, I hope it is evident I try to practice the principles in this book. I am human and will never embody them perfectly, but I do hope my conscious practice of them is visible.

I love you both so much,

Dad

Index